Russell Country

Dedicated to Lavena Lawrence Wolf, artist,
whose presence painted great beauty.

Russell Country

WESTERN COWBOY POETRY

Bette Wolf Duncan

ISBN 0-88839-481-0
Copyright © 2001 Bette Wolf Duncan

Cataloging in Publication Data
Duncan, Bette Wolf.
  Russell country

  Poems.
  ISBN 0-88839-481-0

  1. Russell, Charles M. (Charles Marion), 1864–1926—Poetry.
2. Cowboys—Montana—Poetry. 3. Ranch life—Montana—Poetry.
I. Title.
PS3507.U62R87 2001   811'.6   C2001-910187-2

Printed in Canada—PRINTCRAFTERS

Cover design: Ingrid Luters
Production: Rod Reid, Ingrid Luters
Front cover image: *The Bucker* by C. M. Russell (1904)
Back cover image: *Surprise Attack* by C. M. Russell (1904)

Published simultaneously in Canada and the United States by

HANCOCK HOUSE PUBLISHERS LTD.
19313 Zero Avenue, Surrey, B.C. V3S 9R9

HANCOCK HOUSE PUBLISHERS
1431 Harrison Avenue, Blaine, WA 98230-5005

(604) 538-1114   Fax (604) 538-2262
(800) 938-1114   Fax (800) 983-2262
Web Site: www.hancockhouse.com   *email:* sales@hancockhouse.com

Contents

List of Images

Foreword

Charles M. Russell arrived in the Montana territory in 1880, at the age of sixteen. While he felt he was in virgin land this was not entirely so. The first white men to set foot in the territory were the Verendrye brothers. They were French fur trappers who, in 1742, ventured as far west as the Yellowstone River. It was not until sixty-two years later that the Lewis and Clark expedition passed through the same territory.

Through most of the first half of the 1800s, Montana was inhabited by Indians including Sioux, Crow, Cheyenne, Assinboine, Blackfoot, Flathead, Nez Pierce, Pend d'Oreille, Kootenai and Gros Ventres. Each tribe had their own homeland and hunting grounds. In the fifty years following Lewis and Clark, whites were very cautious about entering this unquestioned Indian domain. A few trappers and fur traders cautiously worked and tracked on the banks of the Missouri, the Yellowstone and their tributaries; but they did so at the mercy of their Indian hosts. Theirs was a dangerous mission in a harsh but beautiful and bountiful country.

It was gold that finally turned Montana white. Gold was found as early as 1850. Thereafter, a series of gold strikes gave rise to boom towns along creeks in the mountainous western portion of the territory. Alder Gulch became Virginia City. Last Chance Gulch later became Helena, the present capitol of Montana. Congress recognized Montana as a territory in 1864, the year of Charlie Russell's birth.

Probably lured by Montana gold, Caleb and George Duncan immigrated to Montana from New Brunswick,

Canada in the early 1880s. Their names are recorded in the 1880 Montana census of Virginia City. Family accounts indicated they later settled in the Judith Basin area near Lewistown. The poem "Shaney Ridge" is based on an actual incident that marred their lives.

At about the same time, Charles Russell was living with a mountain man named Jake Hoover. He was a trapper, hunter and prospector. Hoover was a man of action and skin hunter who sold meat, among other things, to the ranchers who lived along the Judith River. Russell lived with Hoover for about two years; and when he was not working or exploring the country about him, he was painting. Russell later worked as nighthawk and horse wrangler with a Judith Basin outfit.

Charles Russell performed reasonably well as a nighthawk; but he did not underestimate his shortcomings. He admitted to not being much of a roper or rider; but his congeniality around the camp and campfire made up for it. While there were those who found fault with Russell's roping and riding, nobody ever complained about his personality. He was considered to be the most popular "kid" on the range. Many cowboys knew him as Kid Russell.

Caleb Duncan knew Charlie Russell. Caleb later settled in the Pryor Mountain area near the Crow and Cheyenne Indian reservations. (The poem "Fury" is based on an actual incident involving Caleb's wife, Emma, and his first-born son.) Records indicate that both Charles Russell and Frederick Remington spent time in this area and used the terrain as a background for many of their paintings.

Russell Country was home to more than just cowboys. In addition to merchants and professionals there were trappers, loggers, prospectors and other laborers. Of the nearly forty thousand residents of Montana recorded by the 1880 census, more than six thousand lived in and near Helena. Helena had no charter, no paved streets or sewers, but it did have nine hotels, two banks, fifteen lawyers, ten doctors and two undertakers. Saloons and brothels outnumbered all of these significantly and were the boomtown's true measure of prosperity.

Russell recognized that the ways of the Old West were vanishing; and he made it his mission to accurately portray those days as they truly were. In Russell's own words:

> The West is dead my friends
> But writers hold the seed
> And what they sow
> Will live and grow
> Again for those who read.

In this book, Bette Wolf Duncan rides the range on a pen and chronicles a few of the events and people that took place or populated Russell Country.

The Bucker by C. M. Russell (1904)

He'll Make a Cowboy Yet

"You can always tell an Eastern dude,"
I used to hear them say.
"It's not the way he looks or talks.
He thinks a different way."

But give the dude a couple years
of gripping leather reins;
and herding cattle all day long,
across the windswept plains;
of getting bucked off from the horse
and battered, bruised and skinned—
with mouth that's full of prairie grit,
whipped up by flogging wind.

Give the dude a couple years
of forty-plus below;
of struggling to feed cattle
through six-foot drifts of snow;
of praying for an early spring—
just to face some flood,
and gully washers bearing down
on cattle mired in mud.

Give the dude a couple years
of calloused hands and sweat.
A couple years of all of this...
he'll make a cowboy yet.
He'll take the time to look around.
He'll see a circling hawk.
He'll take the time to listen
and he'll hear the prairie talk.

The same old horse he used to cuss,
he'll cherish as a friend.
He'll stoke his fire contented
when the day draws to an end.

Thanksgiving Dinner for the Ranch by Frederic Remington (1888)

Shaney Ridge

They rode into Montana
with their pockets full of poor,
their appaloosa ponies,
and the homespun clothes they wore.
What was it about Shaney Ridge
that drew the brothers there?
Clear springs of mountain water!
They glistened everywhere.

Through icy chills and six foot drifts,
through mud and sleet and mire,
across the range their claim spread out
from Shaney Ridge to Pryor.
None of it was easy—
One crisis spawned another—
but through it all good-natured George
cheered his worried brother.

Winters tortured Shaney Ridge;
but when the sixth one passed,
nature begged forgiveness
and the range thawed out at last.
Caleb's spirit blossomed out
as soon as winter died;
and that spring Caleb left the Ridge
to fetch a promised bride.

When Caleb and his bride returned,
two months had passed them by.
The parching sun was overhead.
The water holes were dry.
The cattle languished on the range;
and George was not around.
As searing as a red-hot brand...
the note that Caleb found.

One night, it seems, that George played cards
with other gambling men.
He lost his cash, his saddle.
He lost his horse.... And then,
he bet the spread at Shaney Ridge.
He lost his bet again!
George wrote that he was leaving...
that someday when he'd earn
enough to buy their holdings back,
then only, he'd return.

It took a while for all the words
to really filter through;
but when they did,
the pain evoked
each curse that Caleb knew.
The dream called Shaney Ridge was gone;
and Caleb had a bride.
So Caleb started over
and hid the rage inside.

Slowly, slowly, years passed by,
as slowly as his ire;
and just as slow, he gained control
of grazing range near Pryor.

What became of brother George?
Caleb never knew.
His bother simply vanished
like Rocky Mountain dew.
Just like the evanescent dew,
impossible to find;
yet when he viewed the Pryor spread,
George often crossed his mind.
He knew he'd chuck the lot of it...
each acre, steer and calf...
just to see George once again
and hear his brother's laugh.

Indian Women Moving by C. M. Russell (1898)

Fury

She lovingly beheld her child...
so tender, pink, and sweet.
Her nine-month journey at an end,
Emma felt complete.
For years, she'd waited for him.
Every night she'd pray
that God would make her fertile...
that she'd have a child one day.
Emma thought a women's place
was in that place called home;
that without a child around her,
she'd always feel alone.

For years, though she was grateful
for the loving man she had,
deep inside, the women there
was "empty-cradle sad."
And when at last, she held her child
and clutched him to her breast,
she thought that God was good to her...
that she'd been doubly blest.

Overhead a V of geese
were winging northward bound.
Down below, with seeds and hoe,
Emma sowed the garden ground.
She placed her cradled infant
beneath a pine with care;
hoping, thus, to shield his eyes
from the sun's bright glare.
Now as she hoed her garden,
some motion caught her eye.
She saw a squaw pick up her child,
then swiftly gallop by.

A group of Crows were winding past
along the Dry Creek trail.
They turned around on hearing
Emma's anguished wail.
She flew just like the geese above,
vaulting fence and streams.
Across the range, the air was wracked
with Emma's wrenching screams.

Usually so gentle,
she was vicious...savage...wild.
She ran and caught the fleeing squaw;
then grabbed her squalling child.

Backing off, the bleeding squaw
fought off a crazed assault;
then lifted up a bloody claw
to urge her foe to halt.
Emma paused; then watched the squaw
ride away alone;
the way she came, was how she left...
without a child...alone.
Forgive the squaw? Impossible!
She knew she never would...
but deep inside, the women there
most surely understood.

The Life Saver by C. M. Russell (1910)

The Durn Contraption

Possessed or just a wild man?
It was pretty hard t' tell.
He flew around the prairie
like some demon outta hell.

He'd fly in that contraption,
(a Model T he named it),
and when he hit some tree or post,
he cursed the thing and blamed it.

The preacher and his missus,
came visiting one day.
The devil drove his Model T
and scared them plumb away.

He honked the durn thing's rooty-toot,
and made the monster roar.
It coughed up fiery clouds a' smoke;
then bellowed out some more.

The team a' horses reared straight up.
The carriage lurched around;
and then the preacher pitched straight out
and slammed into the ground.

It wasn't bible verses
he was yellin' when he hit;
and it wasn't any sermon
that the preacher would admit.

The driver didn't hear it cuz
he flew along so fast.
He hit the fence and took it out;
then swiftly whizzed on past.

Then the durn thing hit the barn.
Y' might have guessed...he blamed it!
"It'll take some time," he said,
"before I've broke and tamed it."

Running Buffalo by C. M. Russell (1918)

Conjuring Back the Buffalo by Frederic Remington (1892)

Sacrifice Cliff

It was The Moon Of Heat Waves
and all the creeks were dry.
Big black birds were gliding,
riding downdrafts in the sky.
The warriors rode toward the cliff—
the children of the long-beaked bird—
in Indian tongue, the Apsaalookes;
Crow, the white man's word.

Every breeze brought whiffs of pine
and pungent scents of gray-green sage.
None of it could ease their pain,
or stem their bitter rage.
Prairie dogs and sage hens
still scrambled wildly on the range;
but piles and piles of buffalo skulls
spoke loudly of the chilling change.
No medicine could conjure back
the herds of buffalo,
that always had provided food
and clothes and shelter for the Crow.

Their hunting days were over
and the life they knew was done.
The Crow would have to start anew;
a new day had begun.
The Crows could fight the soldiers
and the bullets they possessed...
but they couldn't fight the pox-fire
the white men brought out west.

Their village had been scourged by pox
and nearly half were dead.
Montana had been washed by blood
and fields were battle-red.

Blood had seeped into the soil
where now the sagebrush grew;
and blood had stained the memory
of every lodge they knew.

There was blood upon the prairie;
and blood upon the sun.
Tears flowed deep inside them—
but their ride was almost done.
The One Who Had Made Everything
was angry with the Crow.
The tribe owed him a sacrifice
before He'd ease their woes.

The warriors gathered on the Rims
around a rocky bluff.
Perhaps the sacrifice they'd give
that day, would be enough.
With blindfolds on their ponies,
down off the cliff they plunged—
their sacrifice completed
and their tribal debt expunged.

The long-beaked birds were clustered
near the cliff on scraggly trees—
gliding, riding downdrafts...
cutting circles in the breeze.
It was The Moon Of Heat Waves.
The grass was brown and dried.
But the grass turned black
with long-beaked birds,
the day the warriors died.

The Out Post by C. M. Russell (1901)

The Smith No. 3 Mine in the Bearcreek area at Washoe, Montana.

Smith Mine Number Three

Some folks see at evening,
the sinkin' of the sun;
but I live in the Beartooths
and I was never one.
It's not so much the sun that sinks.
The Beartooths climb up high;
and through the day they pierce their way
through distant miles of sky.
At evenin' time they reach the sun;
and there, they stop and pray.
I like to think they'll pray for those
who'll die down here today.

Seventy-seven men came t' work
at Smith Mine Number Three.
Some miners well might leave alive;
but one will not be me.
Four other men were trapped with me.
The four of them are dead.
It doesn't take too smart a' man
t' see what lies ahead.
The mine's smelled foul all this shift.
The shaft on down was gassed.
Someone had an open flame.
The mine shook from the blast.

God! Oh God! Don't leave me
in this Smith Mine Number Three.
My wife is up there waitin'.
Don't take my life from me.
We planned on going into town,
tonight, my wife and I;
to dance and drink and meet with friends.
This ain't no time t' die.
I wish that I could hold again
the hands that waved goodbye;
and see her soft and gentle face,
just once before I die.

There's songs t' sing and jigs t' dance.
This ain't a time for cryin'.
There's trout t' catch and elk t' hunt.
This ain't a time for dyin'.
But then, I guess there'd never be
a time that would be right
t' say goodbye t' all of this
and pass into the night.
There'll never be a time that's right
for givin' up and dyin';
and when I leave my love, I'll go
a' clawin' coal and tryin'.

There's no way out. There's no way in.
The rescuers can't save me.
God! Oh God! Don't take away
this fragile life you gave me.
I guess by now the Beartooths
have climbed up through the sky,
and their snowy peaks are prayin'
as you bless them from on high.
Hear their prayer...and hear my prayer.
Stay with me God I pray.
Have mercy on us miners
who die down here today.

Rescuers with one of the three survivors of Smith Mine. The other seventy-four miners died in the mine on February 27, 1943. Three shifts were working six days a week to meet the coal needs of a nation at war. A number of the Smith No. 3 miners who might otherwise have stayed at home, came to work that day. It was Saturday, and they were getting time-and-a-half. Bill Pelo had a flat tire and John Hodnik overslept. Both just barely made it to go down with the morning shift. Clarence Williams had been sick and his wife asked him to stay home; but he insisted on going to work rather than miss the overtime pay. It was supposed to be Pete Giovetti's last day as a miner. He and his family had saved enough for a small farm and they were moving there the next day. Joe McDonald was also working his last shift as a miner. He was going to report for military service the next Tuesday. A full shift of seventy-seven men reported for work that morning. Of these miners, only three survived.

Stampeded by Lightning by Frederic Remington (1909)

Thunder on the Prairie

It happened down in Kansas
in the cattle drive that year.
We'd driven several thousand head
and Dodge was drawing near.
The men were feeling frisky
and the herd was movin' fine.
Ahead was Dodge and whisky—
woman, poker, wine.

The cattle all were travelin' good.
Each paunch was filled with grass.
The stock had watered three hours back
at Conestoga Pass.
Cows are ploddin' animules;
but scare 'em, they get fast.
A thousand hoofs will jump as one
then swiftly thunder past.

Some folks say a cowboy sings
to calm the skittish steers.
Others say a cowboy sings
to simply please his ears.
But put a cowboy in the dark
and like as not, he'll sing.
The reason matters little.
His song's a soothin' thing.

Rawhide Smith was singin'
as he circled on his rounds.
The cattle seemed t' cotton
to Rawhide's mellow sounds.

> *Whoopee ti yi yea.*
> *git along little dogies.*
> *It's your misfortune*
> *and none a' my own.*

The night had cooled the prairie down.
It baked the whole day long,
but now the dust was kickin' up;
the wind was growin' strong.
Overhead and to the west
ominous black clouds
had formed above the skyline
and draped the moon in shrouds.

The storm was still a long way off;
its rumble barely heard.
The cattle all were layin' quiet;
with very few that stirred.
Save for streaks of lightening
showing cattle now and then,
you'd not have known two thousand steers
were there beside the men.

Then a slashing bolt of lightening
gave the sky a ragged tear;
and a crashing jolt of thunder
exploded in the air.
Rawhide Smith was singin'
"a whoopee ti yi yea."
but while the man was singing,
he was prayin' all the way.
Blinding rain came pelting down,
obscuring all the herd.
You couldn't make out Rawhide;
and his song was barely heard.

The thunder shook the country.
The herd jumped up as one;
and then, without exception,
each steer began to run.
The rain came down with fury,
bombarding every steer.
Rawhide Smith was caught up front;
with cattle in the rear.

We looked around for Rawhide.
His slicker caught our sight.
He was trying to outrun
eight thousand hoofs in flight.
The lightening cast an eerie glow
upon each racing steer.
The prairie shook from pounding hoofs;
while I just shook from fear.

Not till daybreak did we stop;
with Rawhide's fate unknown.
The trail looked like the wreckage
left by Texas 'clones.
The cattle all were smeared with mud,
with tongues all lolling out.

Soon they started feeding
and milling all about.
Where was Rawhide? Not around!
We couldn't find a trace.
It wasn't hard to track in mud;
and we searched everyplace.

And then we saw some yellow
from the slicker Rawhide wore.
We looked and found poor Rawhide
concealed by mud and gore.
Rawhide was a prairie man.
We buried him out there.
Lonesome—yet, not quite alone—
with echoes sounding everywhere.

> *Whoopee ti yi yea.*
> *Git along little dogie.*
> *I've unpacked my bedroll*
> *and found a new home.*

Men of the Open Range by C. M. Russell (undated)

The Rustler's Roost

It long was rumored that a gang
a' rustlers hid out there...
somewhere in the Bighorns—
but none could tell y' where.
They said that way back in those peaks,
by chance, a gang had found—
away from any searching eyes—
a stretch a' hidden ground.

I figured it for nonsense...
some geezer's windy tale.
I'd never been across it
and I'd seen most every trail.
Folks say that I'm a ne'er-do-well;
a no-count saddle tramp...
well, what I am's a mountain man
who jus' prefers t' camp.

While trackin' down some game one day
I came upon a range
that I had never seen before...
which in itself was strange.
To begin with, how I found it
was to climb a granite ledge.
I had t' travel careful
not t' tumble off the edge.

Far below, the canyon walls
were wet from river spray
a' kicked up by the rapids
as they tossed and boiled away.
I was movin' slow and cautious,
a huggin' tight the wall,
when suddenly I came upon
the strangest sight a' all.

On a boulder, overhead,
a rifle barrel gleamed;
and what had seemed secluded,
wasn't what it seemed.
A group a' rifle totin' men
quickly ringed around me
and motioned me t' follow
the one a' them that found me.

He led me to a plateau
with knee-high prairie grass.
Who'd a' thought you'd find such
        range
up in this arid pass?
There were elk up in the north end,
and mountain goats nearby;
and now and then a ring-necked
        pheasant
shot into the sky.

A little bit a' Eden...
it was somethin' for t' see.
The likes a' it were seldom known
by the likes a' me.
There were trout down in the river;
duck and pheasant, lots a' game:
and save the river, no way in
except the way we came.
And you couldn't raft that river;
so what better place t' hide?
You could hole up here forever
and never ride outside.

To a man, the gang all said
they'd long since known about me;
that though I didn't know of them,
they'd seldom been without me.
They'd followed me. They'd searched my tent.
They knew each place I went.
They knew I'd been in prison
and about the stretch I'd spent.
They said that they were short a' men
and needed one more hand;
that if I'd help with cattle,
I was welcome in their band.

They treated me with kindness,
and they mostly showed respect;
and though they boozed quite
    often,
they were mostly circumspect.
I'd known so many others
on the right side a' the law,
who'd left their mean and bitter
    barbs
a stickin' in my craw.

I stayed and tended to the stock
and figured that at least
they weren't as bad as robber barons
rustlin' in the East.
The band would often ride away,
then later ride on back
without leaving in their wake
a single trace or track.

One Spring, they rustled up a herd
and headed for the Chisholm.
Not a one of them returned.
They ended up in prison.
They'll be there for a long, long time...
a dozen years or more...
but I'll be here a' waitin'...
if I don't get caught before.

SOILED DOVES

The Old West was home to more than cowboys. In addition to merchants and professionals there were trappers, loggers, prospectors, miners and other laborers. Most unskilled jobs were beyond the physical strength of the average woman who ventured out onto the frontier. Positions that remained socially acceptable (seamstress, laundress, milliner, waitress, etc.) paid very little. Owners usually tended their own shops; schoolteacher positions were scarce; and few towns lacked a seamstress. Single women who lacked independent financial resources had to make a living in a difficult and rugged man's world. Many unprotected and desperate women turned to prostitution. History records more than a few of these so-called "soiled doves."

Of the nearly forty thousand residents of Montana recorded by the 1880 census, more than six thousand lived in and around Helena. Helena had no city charter, no paved streets or sewers, but it did have nine hotels, two banks, fifteen lawyers, ten doctors, and two undertakers. Saloons and brothels outnumbered all of these significantly, and were the boomtown's true measure of prosperity.

Charlie Russell had grown more devil-may-care as he began his ninth year in Montana; and the saloons and brothels became a second home. Much of his enjoyment was found in the company of a woman whose virtue was negotiable. In Helena, where Charlie spent most of his time when not in Judith Basin, there were at least half a dozen sporting houses employing nearly a hundred girls. Numerous customers reported seeing Charlie's drawings pinned to the walls of brothels, although the consensus is that they were presents, not payments for services rendered.

Just a Little Pleasure by C. M. Russell

Just a Little Series

Russell directed a large portion of his work to local Montana saloons. His bawdy, cow-camp humor was well-received in barrooms where women were not permitted. For the Silver Dollar Saloon in Great Falls, he painted a series of four watercolors that is now referred to as the *Just a Little* series. One of the watercolors, *Just a Little Pleasure* (pictured above) shows a cowboy seated on a prostitute's bed as she pulls off his boots. The titles of these watercolors are a takeoff on a well-known song of the day: *Just a Little Sunshine, Just a Little Rain, Just a Little Pleasure, Just a Little Pain.*

Another risqué painting of Russell's, *Cowboy Bargaining for an Indian Girl*, shows a cowboy holding one finger up to an Indian, apparently offering one dollar for the Indian's daughter. The Indian counters with two fingers. In the background an Indian girl stands with her eyes directed to the ground and her blanket wrapped tightly around her.

Paint Me Red

Lured by Molly's famous face,
the painter stopped by Molly's Place.
There he tarried for a while,
enjoying Molly's painted smile.

But when the tender night was gone,
chased away by jealous dawn,
the painter wanted something more...
he yearned to paint the pretty whore.

Miss Molly wore her working clothes,
and struck a smiling, artful pose.
The painter though, saw so much more
than just the painted smile she wore.

He vowed to paint the grief inside;
and all the tears she tried to hide.
To be precise, he said his goal...
it was to paint Miss Molly's soul.

"Paint me bawdy. Paint me red!
But paint me with a smile," she said.
"Sometimes it's better just to hide
the heartaches carried deep inside.

"I'll pose the way you ask of me...
but leave my soul and sorrows be.
It's fate, not me, that dealt my hand.
I play my cards as best I can.

"Just paint me bawdy. Paint me red.
Paint me on a crimson bed.
It beats the view and hue I knew...
tarpaper shack, bone-chilling blue."

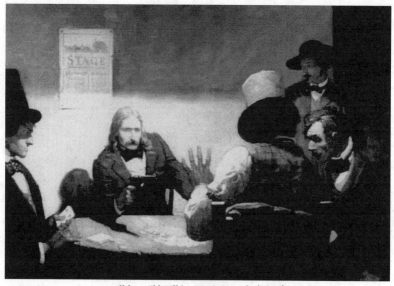

Call by Wild Bill by N. C. Wyeth (1916)

Tex Lafitte

His Pa was from the Bayou,
not far from Thibodaux.
His mother, from El Paso,
by way of Mexico.
Though he was born in Texas,
and considered Texican,
he cursed a lot in Cajun
and his songs were Mexican.

He'd played a lot of poker
from Big D to San Antone.
Sometimes it cost him plenty—
near everything he owned.
But New Orleans was different.
It was good to Tex Lafitte.
He seldom lost a poker game
while down on Bourbon Street.

The wailing horns of Bourbon Street
pulsated in his blood.
He'd sink into their rhythms
as if sucked by bayou mud.
He liked the beat on Bourbon Street.
He liked its boozy blues;
and when he played on Bourbon Street
he'd very seldom lose.

Bourbon Street, he said, was where
his lucky lady stayed.
On Bourbon Street, she held his hand
most every game he played.
The fact is, down on Bourbon Street,
his luck was just the same;
but with more verve and far more nerve,
he played a different game.

One Mardi Gras, a few years back,
it seems that Tex Lafitte
met an East Coast card sharp,
down on Bourbon Street.
The card slick knew most every trick
and tried out quite a few...
but none of it availed him much
because Tex knew them, too.

Tex just plain outplayed him
at every trick he tried.
There wasn't much Tex failed to see;
Nor card the slick could hide.
The stranger played the poker game
as if he'd won a lot;
but when the game was over,
it was Tex that won the pot.

The stranger lost more than the pot.
The stranger lost his cool.
He called Lafitte a dirty cheatin',
two-bit greaser's fool.
He bellowed many curses out;
but kept repeating one.
Lafitte was just a "dirty cheatin'
two-bit greaser's son."

Tex ignored him till the stranger
flashed a loaded gun,
and said that only one of them
would walk when night was done.
Two shots exploded in the air,
and echoed in the street.
One was from the stranger's gun,
one shot was from Lafitte.

The stranger had a crystal ball.
The words he said came true,
that only one of them would walk
when the night was through.
Only one survived the night...
as threatened...only one...
the one he called the "dirty cheatin',
two-bit greaser's son."

The Bull That Brought Him Down

Casey was a rodeo star,
a rider of renown;
and we were proud of Casey
for he came from our small town.
Casey's skills were much admired
by folks across the west.
When it came t' ridin' bulls
he ranked among the best.

Casey could ride any bull;
at least that's what we thought.
Buckles...he'd won many—
and prize money...quite a lot.
His bank account was loaded
and his pockets, always full...
until one day he got the urge
t' ride the Wall Street bull.

Casey was a rodeo star—
a rider of renown;
but in the end it was a bull
that brought poor Casey down.
At first, the ride went easy.
The stock he chose was good,
outperforming others
like the broker said it would.

But then a bear came pouncin' in.
It reared straight up 'n roared.
Before he knew what happened...
Casey's ass was gored.
Now Casey runs from Wall Street bears...
and Wall Street bulls... the same.
He sez' compared to Wall Street,
his rodeo ridin's tame.

Best Wishes Card
by C. M. Russell (1914)

Whiskey Ridin'

From riding bulls and bucking broncs,
he earned a certain fame.
From Canada to Mexico,
his was a well-known name.

"There ain't a bronc that I can't ride,"
you'd often hear him say;
and sometimes he would show with pride
the buckle won that day.

But when the cowboy's ride was through,
whiskey rode on him.
It rode his back and kicked his flank,
and spurred his every limb.

There was no bronc he couldn't ride...
or drink he could refuse;
and in the end, whiskey won...
then every ride he'd lose.

In the end, whiskey won...
whiskey, wine and gin.
He doesn't ride broncs anymore—
but whisky still rides him.

CATTLE COUNTRY TRILOGY

The Sweat Belongs T' Me

The banker owns this ranch of mine...
but all the misery,
and pain and sweat that goes with it—
well, that belongs t' me.
While I might hold the title,
until it's clear and free—
the banker owns the ranch, the stock
and my machinery.
He makes it clear who owns it
when I'm late repaying loans.
While I might own the title,
the rest the banker owns.

Y' take a loan out on your place
when profit's t' be had—
but sooner, more than later,
the economy turns bad.
Recessions and Depressions
always hit the farmers first;
and farmers are the first t' pay
when the bubbles burst.
My grandpa used t' tell me,
"Avoid the mortgage trap....
Y' go t' bed with bankers,
y' end up with the clap."

"Expand...buy new equipment...
y' gotta modernize...."
That's what the Big Boys had t' say.
I thought that they were wise.
And now the banker owns my ranch
and my machinery;
but all the work that goes with them,
well, that belongs t' me.
While I might hold the title,
until it's clear and free—
the banker owns this ranch of mine...
the sweat belongs t' me.

Mad Dog Mean

Mad dog mean the times are
and it just turned snarlin' rough.
It happened just a while ago.
They carted off my stuff.
This ranch has been my family's
for near a hundred years.
The bank's a gonna auction it.
Too bad they can't sell tears.
If only they could sell my tears,
there'd be enough t' pay
back taxes and delinquent loans
and wipe this grief away.

They loaded Grandma's poster bed
her chiffonier and such.
The chances are
that none a' it
will bring too awful much.
The times are mean and ugly...
this day's a snarlin' bitch.
If only I was someone else.
If only I was rich.
The fact is, I ain't none a' that.
I'm just a rancher's wife
who's never known or wanted
another way of life.

If only I could melt away
and join the auction crowd,
and bid on Grandma's poster bed,
and walk with head unbowed.
Great Grandma gave the bed t' her
when she was just a bride.
I watched my grandma make the bed
and polish it with pride.

I've known a lot a' hard times—
but this sure beats all I've seen.
The times have sunk their teeth in me.
It just turned mad dog mean.

Tom and Me

All I ever wanted was
t' ranch on grandpa's place.
It's hard for me acceptin'
that with Tom, that ain't the case.
Tom, he'll be the last one
t' bear the family name.
I never could quite understand...
he didn't feel the same
With me and those before me,
we were fixtures on the land.
With Tom, the ranch means nothin'
but some greenbacks in our hand.
Tom, he wanted somethin' else...
a different life and place.
And Tom was filled with memories
that time could not erase.

He watched while Banion lost his ranch
and everything he owned.
It didn't bring enough t' pay
the funds the bank had loaned.
Recession ate his equity
and left him with a debt
beyond what he could hope t' pay
with prices he could get.
And one day Banion shot himself...
and Tom could not forget.
T' make it ranchin' nowadays
takes more than work and sweat.

Then Tom went off t' college,
and he got himself a job.
He's makin' lots a' money
and he hobnobs with the snobs.
I used t' think I'd never sell.
My sweat's in every clod,
in every furrow on this land;
my life's plowed in the sod.

We always made a livin'—
though I can't say that we thrived.
But still, when others bellied up
Tom and me survived.
But Tom would often urge me
t' blaze some brand new trail;
and come the next inflation,
t' list the ranch for sale.
Now lately, I have wondered;
maybe Tom is right.
This getting' old is somethin'
that is might hard t' fight.
My back and joints are tellin' me
that this time I can't win.
There comes a time for givin' up—
a time for givin' in.

Last Chance or Bust by C. M. Russell (1900)

Prairie Woman

In the middle of some nowhere,
she loomed larger than the plain,
giving it a tender splendor,
sweeter than the prairie rain.
Selfless prairie woman!
Though often tired, she hid it.
She had a lot of love to plow
and zealously she did it.

She went from dawn to weary dusk
and seldom took a rest;
and when she did, she'd likely hold
a baby to her breast.
She had a million chores to do.
I don't know how she did them.
She must have felt a million aches;
but when she did, she hid them.

She'd feed the cows and chickens,
and help to plant the crop.
She'd peel a tree of apples,

and can until she'd drop.
Repugnant as the chore might be,
she'd manage to get through it;
like emptying the chamber pot...
someone had to do it.

Selfless prairie woman!
She seldom took a rest.
Her family thrived on well-cooked meals,
and clothing that was clean and pressed.
She scrubbed the clothes with lye soap
till her weary hands were red.
She'd scrub them on a scrub board
till, at times, her knuckles bled.
Selfless prairie woman!
You'd seldom see her sitting;
and if you did, you'd likely see her
darning socks or knitting.
Selfless prairie woman!
Bigger than the sky above!
She gave the plains a tender bloom
and nourished it with love.

Wyoming Cattle Drive, Dewey Vanderhoff photo

The Cattle Drive

I'm a cattle drivin' cowboy
who rides 18 wheeler rigs.
My job's a haulin' cattle...
and it sure beats haulin' pigs.

My rig's revved up and roarin';
it's all gassed up and greased.
With a load a' bawlin' cattle,
I'm headin' for the East.

I figure that I'm drivin'
with a ton a' sirloin steaks;
but none a' them 'r for me...
ain't got the dough it takes.

I'll stop somewhere fer coffee
and a chunk a' apple pie,
and dream about them beef steaks
I can't afford t' buy.

Sometimes jus' t' pass the time
I think about the past;
and wish them days were back again—
and this time, that they'd last.

Sometimes when I'm on the road
it gets t' feelin' real...
my hands are back a' holdin' reins
and not some steerin' wheel.

And I'm back upon a saddle
and not this driver's seat.
I'm a' flyin' not on 18 wheels
but on some horse's feet.

I've got an air conditioned rig
and soft upholstered seat;
and outside it's a' blisterin' hell
and folks 'r wiltin' in the heat.

I've got a bed inside the cab.
It's comfortable, of course...
but still I'd chuck the lot a' it
t' be back on a horse.

I'm a cattle drivin' trucker;
but I wish that I could be
back on the range a' herdin' steers
with a good horse under me.

The Rancher's New Computer

After riding through the plains,
the tumbleweeds and sage,
he'd come back home and ride into
the new computer age.

He entered his computer
and the rancher felt the same
as Lewis and Clark must have felt
while crossing western plains.

The rancher, like the two of them,
rode through the vast unknown,
to find a strange and distant range
a million miles from home.

Alone, uncertain, hesitant,
he fought his own "Star Wars."
He crossed into a surreal world
as alien as Mars.

Exaggerated? "No," he'd say,
"In essence it's quite true.
It's like a science fiction book
the things this box can do."

Wanted by Rob Robinson (undated)

Wanted, Living or Dead

The vista was wrong. He didn't belong
any where on this sage-crested prairie.
Jones longed for the fogs and the salt-water bogs;
and the thought that he'd die here was scary.

He missed sailing ships and the fierce whaling trips;
and he'd die for some stout Boston ale.
Any port is a jail when your heart yearns to sail
and his yearned for schooners and whale.

But he'd killed a man; then left Boston and ran.
Bounty hunters were hot on his trail.
He could ride with the best and was safe in the west...
and it sure beat some dank Boston jail.

Now at high noon, in the Pryor Creek saloon,
a dude with a scar slammed the door...

From the East Coast, Jones guessed,
from the way the dude dressed,
and the cut of the clothes that he wore.
With a poster that read, "WANTED, LIVING OR
    DEAD,"
he glanced at each man in the place.
Jones faced the bar. Thus the dude with the scar
saw his back and not Jones's anguished face.

With guns on his hips, and Jones's name on his
    lips,
he flashed an old picture of Jones.
The sheriff was there. He leaned back in his chair,
and suppressed his annoyance and groans.
Bounty hunters he cursed. Their kind was the
    worst;
and Jones seemed a quite decent sort…
Didn't cause any trouble like some of the rubble
who shot up the town just for sport.
The worn poster read, "WANTED LIVING OR
    DEAD."
The sheriff asked what the man did.
The dude turned his head to the sheriff and said,
"He shot a rich banker's kid.
His Pa's worth a lot; and will pay all he's got.
Doesn't matter that Sonny shot first."

Said the sheriff, "Could be…
but I'd search by the sea.
There's no ships or water out here.
The closest you'll get to anything wet
is a mug of the bartender's beer.
It strikes me as strange
that you'd search on the range.
Frisco's more like it, I'd say.
Sailor's like that flock to Frisco like rats
and hole up in dives near the bay."

Then the dude showed a card;
and the sheriff looked hard.
The postmark read PRYOR CREEK as feared.
Jones still used his name;
but his looks weren't the same.
He'd aged; and he'd grown a full beard.
"Take a look round the place.
Do you see any face
that looks like the picture you've brought?
Put down your gun. Do you see anyone
that looks like the picture you've got?"

The last time I heard, no one breathed a word
(and by now, it's been nearly ten years).
The dude caught a stage, leaving Pryor and the
     sage;
and Jones is still rounding up steers.

The Big Die-up

In the two years after Charley Russell arrived in the Judith Basin area of the Montana territory, the country filled with ranchers and their stock. The area was covered with a mixture of hardy, nutritional grasses. Speculators abounded. At this time Russell was working as a nighthawk for a Horace Brewster; and as such, his duties included the safekeeping of several hundred mounts without the benefit of fences or help from sleeping comrades.

In the winter of '86 and '87, the first cold front hit in November. More storms followed in December. A foot and a half of snow fell between Thanksgiving and Christmas. What little hay they had, most ranchers fed to their horses. In the meantime, the cattle drifted from the frozen high ranges to the bottom land and the sheltered coulees. There was no food there but willows. The first chinook arrived in January, with just enough warming to melt the snow on top. Then it turned cold. On February 3 and 4 one of the worst blizzards in memory set in. The snow crusted. The chinook had succeeded in sealing the ground with a layer of ice, which the cattle hooves could not penetrate. Before he died, Russell dictated to a stenographer this account of what happened.

> The winter of '86 and '87 all men will remember. It was the hardest winter the open range ever saw. An awful lot of cattle died. The cattle would go in the brush and hump up and die there. They wasn't rustlers. A horse will paw and get grass, but a cow won't. Then the wolves fattened on the cattle.... Now I was living at the OH Ranch that winter. There were several men there, and among them was Jesse Phelps, the owner of the OH. One night, Jesse Phelps had

got a letter from Louie Kaufman, one of the biggest cattlemen in the country, who lived in Helena, and Louie wanted to know how the cattle was doing, and Jesse says to me, "I must write a letter to Louie and tell him how tough it is." I was sitting at the table with him and I said, "I'll make a sketch to go with it." So I made one, a small water color about the size of a postal card, and I said to Jesse, "Put that in your letter." He looked at it and said, "Hell, he don't need a letter, this will be enough."

On the bottom of a box, Russell completed one of his most memorable paintings. In gray and brown and black colors, he painted a single steer with a Bar R branded on its hip. It was standing in deep snow with horns crooked and eyes hollow. Its backbones and every rib were showing. Wolves lurked in the background; and the steer's tail had been chewed to a nub. The forlorn steer stands lonely and alone. Russell titled it *Waiting for a Chinook (The Last of the 5000)*.

Louie Kaufman gave the painting to a saddle-maker friend of Russell's, Ben Roberts. Roberts displayed it on the wall of his shop where it collected grime for the next twenty-five years. Eventually, Roberts got the idea of reproducing it; and he printed postcards by the thousands.

A copy of the painting follows, along with an interpretive poem, "The Lonely One" (written in the rhyme scheme employed by Robert Frost in "Stopping by Woods on a Snowy Evening"; ie., aaba, bbcb, ccdc, etc.). The poem was intended to be as gaunt and stark as the emaciated steer in the painting.

Waiting for a Chinook—The Last of the 5000 by C. M. Russell (1887)

The Lonely One (Montana, 1886–1887)

There used to be 5000 head.
Now there was only one instead...
a single steer...the lonely one...
the only one that wasn't dead.

Another day had just begun.
The steer's was dim and almost done.
A wolf pack gathered, lurking near—
but he was weak... too weak to run.

The wolf pack stalked the lonely steer...
almost gone, and filled with fear...
too weak to move...no place to go...
a victim of that fiendish year.

So gaunt and thin, with bones that show...
no food and forty plus below...
no letup in the bitter storm...
just slogging through more ice and snow.

Sleepy now and growing warm...
beyond the reach of further harm.
His torment done, the lonely one
walked toward the warm, warm sun.

The Free Trapper by C. M. Russell (1911)

Mountain Man
(The Legend of Earl Durand)

The mountain moon's a ridin'
on the stallion of the night;
with snowflakes softly glidin' down
its flowing mane of light.
The midnight winds are siftin'
through the driftin' flakes of snow;
and you can hear 'em whistlin'
through the pine trees as they blow.
Some think my trail's a lonely one...
without a soul in sight;
with no one there t' talk to
save the wailin' winds of night.
But what I am's a mountain man.
I do jus' fine out here.
I've mostly slept beneath the sky.
I feed on elk and deer.

Good friends, these mountains are t' me...
the kindest ones I've known;
and when I'm in these mountains,
I'm never quite alone.
I like t' hear the whisperin'
of a gentle mornin' breeze;
and listen t' the birdsong
that's pourin' from the trees.

A posse's out there after me
with bullets by the score.
But they won't take this mountain man
like they did before.
I've gotta keep on ridin' now,
and hidin' from the law....
avoidin' men, evading them—
holed up in some dark draw.

I killed game outta season,
but the reason for my flight
is, when they jailed me for it,
I killed a guard one night.

I couldn't breath...I couldn't think...
went crazy in that cell.
It stripped me of my reason;
and delivered me t' hell.
No longer was I human,
but an animal confined;
without the human faculties
that bless the human mind.

A mountain man is what I am...
unfettered, wild and free—
and nevermore will prison bars
mock the man in me.
Nor will they hang this mountain man.
Of this I'm sure for I've
resolved that they will never take
this mountain man alive.

And when their bullets find me—
as their bullets surely will—
a free, unfettered mountain man
is what they're gonna kill.
The mountain moon's a' ridin'
on the stallion of the night;
with snowflakes softly slidin' down
its silvery tail of light.
When I am dead and buried
and this flight from terror ends,
I'll mount that coal-black stallion
and rejoin my mountain friends.

WILD MUSTANGS

Horse Wrangler by Olaf Wieghorst (undated)

What better symbol of the spirit of the Old West is there than the wild horse? Today, millions identify with its indomitable spirit. The modern horse was introduced to North America by Spanish explorers in the sixteenth century. Horses that escaped or were released from captivity by Indians or settlers banded together to form large mixed herds. These were the first "wild horses." Unlike domestic animals, these wild horses are on their own during the winter months and must forage on rugged and inhospitable terrain. Bands of wild horses survive in places few other creatures would call home.

With the emergence of European markets for horse meat, and domestic markets for pet food and chicken feed, wild horses began disappearing in large numbers from the western range. Capturing and transporting wild horses for profit became a thriving business for some; and their methods were often brutal. Ultimately the public outcry led to the passage of THE WILD HORSE AND BUREAU ACT OF 1971. Wild horses that roam public land are now protected under this act.

Free as the Wild River Rapids

He was wild as the crest on the rapids;
and swift as the eagles on high.
When you saw him race 'cross the prairie,
you'd swear he had wings and could fly.

The cowboys all called him The Ghost Horse.
You'd glimpse him and then he'd be gone.
He'd appear of a sudden like sunrise...
then vanish like dew after dawn.

A horse like none other—that stallion—
and I wished that just once 'ere I die
I could climb to the top of Olympus
and mount that black devil and fly.

He was wild as the winds of Dakota;
and just as resistant to rope.
I'd tried now for years to lasso him;
and each time he quashed every hope.

I chased him one time to the Bighorns...
to a place that was known to the Crow...
it was known to the Crow and few others;
but by chance, one that I'd come to know.

It was bounded by river on one side
and on two sides, a steep granite wall.
Between river rapids and granite...
there was only one exit—that's all.

And I stood at the mouth of that exit...
I had the horse cornered at last.
I figured the days he could best me
were truly a thing of the past.

Like a war horse snortin' in battle,
with the wind a whippin' the plain,
the stallion was racing the rapids
with the wind tugging hard at his mane.

Inextricably part of the picture...
the rapids, the plain and the wind;
all free, unrestrained and unconquered—
but this time I had the horse pinned.

Then the stallion turned off a' sudden;
and, I swear, looked me straight in the eye—
then like Pegasus high on Mount Helicon,
he spread out his wings and flew by.

I was waiting and ready for battle.
I let out a blood curdling whoop.
With all the skill I could muster,
I aimed and threw out my loop.

I had waited so long for this moment
and practiced for years on my throw—
but the horse was as quick as the lightning;
and I was a tad bit too slow.

He was free as the wild river rapids...
no kin of a peaceful, slow stream....
Maybe God meant the rapids to race free
and for me to just back off and dream.

When Cows Were Wild by C. M. Russell (1902)

Herd Quitter by C. M. Russell (1897)

Almost a Cowboy

He was almost a cowboy...
almost, but not quite.
Poor Jones couldn't seem
t' do the job right.
He could castrate the bulls
and brand the new steers...
but not like the cowpokes
who'd done it for years.

He'd average with pokes
when it came to his looks;
but one glance would tell you
his place was with books.
"Boston," they called him;
then ragged about beans,
and how he looked baked
in his Boston-bought jeans.

One roundup, he rode out
with two other pokes.
Like always poor Jones
was the butt of their jokes.
Their job? Rope Big Ugly,
and bring the bull in;
corral him, castrate him,
and brand the brute's skin.

The lasso of one poke
caught Big Ugly's horn.
The bull lunged. In seconds
the man was airborne.
Up like an eagle—
then down like a rock!
The poke hit the dust
like a winged, squawking hawk.

He was raked through the cactus,
the rocks and the sage.
As the bull snaked the cowboy,
both bellowed with rage.
The loop that Jones threw
went sadly awry...
a bit too much snap,
a little too high.

Meanwhile the bull
gored the second poke's horse.
It bucked and the cowboy
pitched forward with force.
The bull charged toward him
with blood in his eyes—
and a look that said,
"Pray—and then say your goodbyes."

The man read his eyes
and said a quick prayer,
but Boston Baked Jones
was the only help there.
Too bridled and gun-shy.
Not grisly or tough.
Just half of a cowboy...
not nearly enough.
But Jones acted fast.
He was awkward, but quick.
He threw out loop two,
and this toss did the trick.

He lassoed Big Ugly,
and jerked the rope tight;
but the bull was part lightening—
the other part, fight!
Though short on the skill,
he was long on the luck.
When the bull shot up skyward
another loop struck.

The two cowboys made it,
though covered with mud;
with flesh skinned like bark,
and dripping with blood.
They didn't call Jones
half a cowboy again.
It was cowboy... and then some...
that saved those two men.

Stagecoach by C. M. Russell (bronze, 20 x 45 in.)
This bronze sculpture is an unfinished work of Russell's, whose original model was made of wax, plaster, cloth, leather, string, metal and paint. A foundry eventually made six bronzes of it.   Caleb Barber photo

Charlie Russell's Stagecoach

Charlie Russell's stagecoach...
I polish it with pride;
and every little now and then
I hop aboard and ride.

I found it in an art store
in Nebraska years ago.
Since then, I guess I've ridden
a million miles or so.

Sometimes I go to Deadwood;
sometimes to Pryor Creek.
I hitch a ride on Russell's coach
a couple times a week.

I can almost hear the passenger
and driver on the coach,
talking to each other
each time that I approach.

For sure, I hear the coach wheels
creakin' 'neath the load;
and I can smell the heavy dust
rising from the road.

Six horses strain to hold the coach
from hurling down the hill.
It never does. The driver reins
the six of them with skill.

So real, the figures in the coach—
a lady and three men—
that when you take a seat inside,
they come to life again.

The geezer spins a windy
and the lady feels disgust
at the tales the coot is spinning
and the way the varmint cussed.

When suddenly some bandits
from the painting on the wall,
block the road, wave their guns,
and threaten one and all.

They empty all our pockets
and take the lady's broach;
then rifle through the carpetbags
strapped upon the coach.

The bandits leave us penniless;
but though we felt distressed,
things perk up the farther that
we travel through the west.

I wonder if old Charlie knew
when sculpting it in wax,
just how many passengers
would follow in his tracks;
or that the coach, when forged in brass,
would ride the range again,
transporting back in time and place,
a myriad of men.

Whose Meat by C. M. Russell (1913)

Caleb's Lament
(1890)

Except for some beans and a tad bit of flour,
the larder was pretty much bare.
Just bannock and beans...
then more bannock and beans.
That's pretty much all that was there.
He found himself dreaming of venison stew;
and while he liked elk, any wild game would do.
He was snowed in and growing quite wolfy and gaunt.
The meat was long gone and the dreamin' a taunt.

That winter he'd suffered through storm after storm
In fact, it was just one long blizzard that year.
You couldn't see much past the nose on your face,
much less to track down an elk or a deer.
Finally, it happened! The storm-maker tired.
He'd run out of wind. He needed a rest.
At last you could see them against a clear sky...
the prongs of the Bighorns...each snow covered crest.

With a pack horse, a prayer, and his Grandfather's gun,
he lit out with elk on his mind.
While snowdrifts were high, the trails were quite clear;
and the weather for huntin' as good as you'll find.
The old flintlock was old when the old man was born.
It was Caleb's after he died.
He kept it beside him; and most every day,
he polished the flintlock with pride.
But the rifle was old, and long past its prime...
just barely enough for a deer.
It didn't pack lead any distance at all.
You had to be standing quite near.

Caleb thought of the poster that some time ago,
he'd nailed to the wall by his bed.
"The new HENRY rifle... The best in The World...
Without Equal...," the circular said.
He was thinking of this when he saw on the ledge
a large Bighorn ram standing close to the edge.
Rugged and regal... with statuesque grace...
with horns curving back from the animal's face;
too splendid to kill...too special to eat...
but not when you're hungry and craving some meat.

Caleb aimed the old flintlock.
He'd have just one shot.
Though as good of a marksman as most,
until he could shoulder a much better gun,

he'd have little reason to boast.
But he was in luck! One shot was enough!
But then suddenly piercing the air,
by the side of the ram, with a menacing look,
was a massive and mean-looking bear.

What can you do when you're armed with a gun
that just barely cuts it with deer?
Forget the old gun... and just simply run,
and hope that there's some shelter near.
The bear gave a sign that said, "Mister, it's mine!"
Caleb fled, though it stuck in his craw.
By rights it was his...that miserable griz...
but possession's nine-tenths of the law.

Shadow of an Eagle

The shadow of an eagle's wings
racing 'cross the mountain side—
I saw it sweep the valley floor,
then pierce the golden sun and soar—
the day that Grandpa died.

I hiked to Grandpa's special place—
a place, he said, for chasing dreams—
where you can leave the world and rest
and fish awhile in silver streams.
He told me of the days of old.
He showed me how he panned for gold.

A shadow skimmed across the stream
that Grandpa panned so long ago—
the place he stopped to chase a dream...
where golden nuggets wink and glow.
He liked to watch the eagles fly
and pierce the blaze of burning sky.
"You see them eagles overhead;
I'd like to fly like them," he said.

The shadow of an eagle's wings
racing 'cross the mountain side—
I saw it glide through open space,
then land at Grandpa's special place—
the day that Grandpa died.

Prospecting for Gold, sketch by C. M. Russell (undated)

Just a Little Rain by C. M. Russell

Rainbow Ridin'

Maybe come tomorrow
I'll ride into the dawn;
and all the rain that's peltin' me
will let up and be gone.
But I'm grateful now for thunder
and the blinding drops of rain,
for when you're rainbow ridin'
they help to ease the pain.

So many times I rode away
and every time I swore
I wouldn't rainbow ride again
like I'd done before.
But then I'd get a letter,
or we'd share a kiss or two...
enough to keep me rainbow ridin'
like I'd always do.

There isn't any rainbow's end...
I found no pot of gold;
but just the rain a' beatin' down
and wind a' growin' cold.
It's only an illusion
paintin' colors on the rain.
It's only self-delusion
paintin' rainbows on the brain.

Maybe come tomorrow
I'll be ridin' in the sun—
maybe come tomorrow
when this rainbow ridin's done.
But I'm grateful now for thunder
and the blinding drops of rain.
For no one knows you're crying
when you're ridin' in the rain.

The Devil's Down in Cheyenne

The devil's down in Cheyenne.
He's red-eyed, raw and mean;
with a whip unreal, two swords of steel,
and the wrath of hell between!

I've ridden bulls from Lethbridge
all the way to San Antone;
but that black, black-hearted devil's
in a class all of his own.

He swallowed up a cyclone.
It's in his belly still.
There's just one thought that devil's got;
and that one's shoutin' "KILL."

The devil's down in Cheyenne;
and though I rode him well,
I wasn't any match for
two thousand pounds from hell.

He left me down in Cheyenne
in a crimson pool a' gore.
The devil's still in Cheyenne—
but I don't ride bulls no more.

Lane Frost statue by Chris Navarro at the Cheyenne Frontier Days Old West Museum. Frost, the 1987 World Champion Bull Rider, was killed by a bull named Taking Care of Business, at the 1989 Cheyenne Frontier Days Rodeo.

Rodeo Rider by W. H. Dunton (1908)

Sidesaddle Friends (1890)

What would her friends think?
A woman who'd ride
not lady-like, with her legs to one side;
but instead, like a man
with legs hanging astride.

The prim code that ruled the Victorian age
had been buried out west
'neath the cactus and sage.
What would her friends think?
She cared not a whit
that her Eastern companions
would fault her for it.

Her friends never raced
with the eagles on high;
or soared on the wings of a horse
'neath the sky.
They were scared to be different;
and dared not to try.
How sad observed Emma...
her friends couldn't fly.

She'd live out her life
in the way she though best.
Let the East stay out East.
This was the West!

The Sweetest Thing on Wheels

My brand-new car don't please Cale
the way this pickup does.
He's always thought this truck a' mine's
the sweetest wheels there was.
Where Grandma backed into the barn,
it's dented up and scratched;
and where a bull gored up the hood,
the holes were poorly patched.
But give this truck a body job...
a brand new coat of paint...
he'll love it like it was one,
though a brand new truck it ain't.

So spruce it up...fix every dent...
fix every dent but one—
the dent upon the fender
that it got from Cale's home run.
I got that at a baseball game.
I should a' had more sense,
but I parked the truck a few yards past
the center outfield fence.
The District High School Championship—
at the top of inning nine,
the Bulldogs were behind by one—
with the Championship on line.
The other team came up to bat,
and increased their lead by two.
The score was 9 to 7 when
the other team was through.

But then the Bulldogs came t' bat.
The lead-off batter walked.
The second batter took a base
when the pitcher slipped and balked.

But the next batter...he struck out;
and the fourth one hit a fly.
It was then that Caleb came t' bat
and kissed that ball goodbye.
It sailed clear past the center field...
and whizzed across the fence.
It smashed into the pickup
With a force that was immense.

I've never cared about that dent...
don't mind that dent at all...
I wouldn't take a million
for the dent caused by that ball.
So don't repair that banged up dent.
Leave it like y' found it.
And when y' paint this pick up truck,
well just y' paint around it.
Caleb's gonna get this truck—
beat-up dent and all,
from a man who's mighty proud t' know
the kid that smacked that ball.

Letter to "Friend Berners" by C. M. Russell (1915)

Charles M. Russell was often called the "word painter." He painted stories in his pictures; and sometimes he painted advice. He once wrote a letter about a sick friend. In it he painted a mountain goat. In his unique brand of English and spelling, he wrote this:

> Old John like the animal above is in a dam dangiros place but the goat don't think so and if I can make my friend feel like the goat I believe hel come across the bad pas.

Russell's timeless advice is the basis for the following poem, but this time with a modern theme.

The Pitcher and the Picture

The game had gone from bad to worse.
He'd lost his pitching touch.
His team might win...without him!
At least, he thought as much.
He sat inside the dugout,
Besieged by troubling doubts.
Not only did his pitching stink...
He'd bombed and just struck out.

He thought about the game
and all the things that he'd done wrong.
His curve ball was flat!
His speed wasn't there!
And his spit and his fire were all gone.
At the top of the sixth
his team came to bat.
They'd fallen behind by three runs
But with a spell of good luck
and just plain old pluck—
      they now led by a total of one.
It was up to the other team's batters right now—
and with the top of the lot yet to bat.
So far this season, his bullets were gone;
And he wondered just where they were at.
In the innings before, they'd zinged quite a few.
It seemed like the harder he tried,
the harder they hit; the more his team quit;
and the more that his bullets all died.

    Demoralized now!
      With these thoughts in his head,
        he thought of the picture
          pinned up by his bed.

"You can do it my friend. Just believe that you can."
These were the words of the "word painter" man.
He painted a mountain goat standing up high
on a scant narrow ledge that pierced clouds in the sky.
The goat stood alone in a small narrow niche,
that was carved in a cliff with a vertical pitch.
The picture instilled one with wonder and doubt:
How could the goat get there or climb its way out?
Such a dangerous place...but the goat didn't scare!
He believed in himself and the path that was there.
The painting inferred, "There's a path way up high.
You can climb like the goat if you've courage to try."

His team took the field, as he took the mound.
"Batter up," he heard the ump call.
He thought of the painting and pictured the ram;
but the first pitch he threw was a ball.
From then on he threw one strike after strike.
He threw the first batter out.
And with the next batter, who likewise struck out,
he struck out each lingering doubt.
He could do it! He knew it—
and that's what he did.
The rest of the game he was hot!
He stood up and threw like the pitcher he knew
and not like the bomb he was not.
His team won the game; and he left the game
with a smile that transfigured his face.
In his mind the goat had discovered the path,
and climbed to a glorious place.

NATE CHAMPION AND THE JOHNSON COUNTY WAR

Drawing of Nate Champion by Richard Florence

In 1858, Nate Champion was born in Texas. He migrated from there to Kaycee, Wyoming, where he worked as a top hand for many ranches in the area. He is described as a good-looking man who was known for his honesty and forthrightness; and he was considered to be a top cowboy. He had many friends among the cowboys and small ranchers in the area. He was not a man you could intimidate and he was handy with guns.

Champion was blackballed for striking out on his own and claiming mavericks (unbranded cattle of uncertain ownership) on the open range. In Wyoming during the 1880s and 1890s, members of the posh "Cheyenne Club" dominated the state's cattle industry. With various lawmen, state commissions and judicial officers in their pockets, they believed that they could get away with anything—and they did for years.

While the cattle boom lasted, the problem of mavericks was largely ignored. Many small ranches started out with a herd of mavericks. During 1885, the value of herds suffered a deflation in value, followed by a depression in 1886 and the devastating winter of 1886–1887, during which the herds were literally decimated. The cowboys found themselves out of work; and when they tried to start a small spread on their own, they were blacklisted by the large ranchers and could not find employment. They were even refused those courtesies then common on the range: they were not allowed a camp meal or allowed to bed down on the range with the big outfits.

The cattle barons formed the Wyoming Stock Growers Association in an effort to control the range. They sought to control the ownership of the cattle and the markets for them. Those attempting to resist or to claim mavericks were labeled as rustlers and thieves. In desperation, the small cattlemen and homesteaders of the Powder River country formed an organization of their own, the Northern Wyoming Farmers and Stock Growers Association. At that time, Nate Champion had a spread on the middle fork of the Powder River, known as the KC ranch. He was one of the leaders of this group. His partner and friend was Nick Ray.

The small cattlemen and homesteaders announced their intention of holding their own roundup anywhere and any time they pleased. They insisted that they were not "rustlers" just because they homesteaded land in the cattle country; and that they had as much right to the mavericks as the big ranchers. Hard times and hard feelings continued, fueled by the killings of men and woman labeled as "rustlers" by the cattle barons.

The Wyoming Stock Growers Association (whose members, for the most part, were also members of the Cheyenne Social Club) saw that their spasmodic efforts were not doing any good. They felt a large-scale assault, even one that was in defiance of the law, was essential. They made plans to invade Johnson County. On April 5, 1892, a three-car special train carrying 25 Texas gunmen recruited in Denver, pulled into Cheyenne and was coupled to another three-car special train carrying horses, wagons, ammunition, dynamite and supplies. Another 24 men recruited in Wyoming boarded this train. The 49 men in this combined band called themselves "the Regulators"; and they carried with them a list compiled by the cattle barons containing the names of enemies to be eliminated. Nate Champion was included on the list.

The poem "The Powder River War" was inspired by historical accounts of the Johnson County Range War and Nate Champion. Names and some details vary. Some historians point out that Champion and the small ranchers were really rustlers rounding up stray cattle. Other historians point out that the cattle barons were just greedy and did not want competition. Whatever else Champion may have been, all historians agree that he was the man who broke the back of "the Regulators" and stalled the Johnson County Range War by his stand at the Powder River. Nate Champion was killed in 1892, at the age of thirty-four. He is buried in the Willow Grove Cemetery in Buffalo, Wyoming. Nick Ray is buried nearby.

Nate Champion 1858–1892

The Powder River Range War

Where the Powder River races
with the eagles in the sky;
And washes off the traces
of the drinking herds nearby;
where canyon walls and waterfalls
box in a range that hid
the cattle and the canyon
of the man called Kaycee Kid;
it was here, just past the marshes
where the river overflowed,
that the Powder River War was fought
with two against a train-load.

Two cowboys facing off against
a train of well-armed men;
all hired by those that called the shots
in Cheyenne, way back then.
Vast fortunes had been made by most.
These cattle barons thrived.
Though over-stocking was a threat,
most all of them survived.
Why not? They held Wyoming
firmly in their grasp;
most all the courts and lawmen there
helped steel their hawkish clasp.

The "open range" was open...
but to them and them alone
And all the mavericks on it...
that was stock they sought to own.
So let some wayward waddie
claim an orphan steer or steed,
a rustler's what they'd call him;
then they'd hang him for the deed.
They hung 'em fast and hung 'em high

for all their friends to see—
and many were the cowboys found
a' dangling from a tree.

The range was *de jure* open...
a law they all opposed.
With courts in hand, they owned the land.
It was *de facto* closed.

With the river fast erasing
all their tracks left on the ground,
walking forms were staking out
the waking world around.
Inside the cabin, yellow sparks
were leaping from the wood
and falling from the fireplace
to the floor where Kaycee stood.
His thoughts were focused on the sparks...
he ought t' get a screen...
while all the while the shadows stalked,
silent and unseen.

When the coffee started boiling.
his partner, Jake, got up.
The coffee smelled so campfire good,
he poured himself a cup.
Still half asleep, he heard outside
his dog's disruptive howls.
"Old Blue," he thought, "must see a wolf,
a' judgin' from his growls."
Kaycee grabbed his Henry
when he heard the barking dog;
and rammed it through some crumbling chinking,
shrinking from a log.

He'd heard about the Barons' plans...
about their hired guns;
and of the men they wanted dead,
he knew that he was one.
Now it was clear to Kaycee
what upset the barking dog...
the Barons' sharp-eyed shadows
that were shooting all around.

The bullets started ripping through
the door, the window pane;
and when Blue's frantic barking stopped,
Jake figured he'd been slain.

He'd herded sheep and steers with Blue
across the range for years;
and dust kicked up by casings
brought a multitude of tears.
Kaycee saw Jake moving
through the corner of his eye.
He was reaching for his rifle
as the bullets zinged nearby.

One moment Jake was cursing
and crawling past the door.
A couple seconds later,
he was sprawling on the floor.
His blood gushed out profusely.
He was bleeding from the head.
A couple seconds later
Kaycee saw that Jake was dead.
Jake had been his partner
and the finest man he'd known.
For years, they both had dreamed about
the ranch they'd one day own.

Kaycee cursed the crooked scales
where wealth weighed more than right;
where justice was no longer blind
for gold restored her sight.
He couldn't bring his partner back,
but by Gawd he could see
that when they came to bury him
he'd have some company.
His rifle roared defiantly...
rounds of bullets soared.
Inside, outside the cabin,
the blazing rifles roared.

As bullets dropped around him;
like striking balls of hail,
he heard them whistle past him...
till one pierced him like a nail.

The blood gushed from his shoulder,
but Kaycee kept right on.
He fired until the shadows
were lifeless or withdrawn:
without regard for life or limb,
trepidation free,
oblivious of pain or blood,
resigned to what would be.

Suddenly, his eye was drawn
to something past the porch.
A man rose up and threw it...
a brightly glowing torch.
He heard it hit the cabin wall
a few feet from the door;
and somehow now, none of it
mattered anymore.

For awhile the Kid hung on,
fighting to the end,
his rifle smoking, furnace-hot,
and thinking of his friend.
Then when the raging cabin fire
was licking on his skin,
he ran outside to finish
what he knew he couldn't win.
The Barons came to bury him.
He paid back what they gave.
He took a dozen men or more
with him to the grave.

Where the Powder River's chasing
after herds a' racing by,
and overhead the eagles
skim across the Western sky,
that's where Kaycee's buried,
and every now and then,
in the wind, you'll hear him whistling
to his maverick herd again.

The Gunfighters by C. M. Marshall (undated)

Fast Finger Finnegan

The cowboys all jawed as they'd gather
at Fast Finger Finnegan's wake.
And as they viewed his cadaver,
they called him a four-flushin' fake.
His draw...not as fast as reputed...
in fact, not as fast as their own.
And the stories they'd heard, they refuted...
all false, or at least, overblown.

It was said that his draw was the fastest
and sorry's the men that dared scoff.
It was said that at least twelve had tried him...
and that Finnegan finished them off.
But the talk of his fast draw was just that...
just talk without basis in fact,
for he was a wily ole' polecat—
and a fast draw was just what he lacked.

He bluffed them all out and succeeded
in flaming their unfounded fears.
A lightening quick draw's what he needed.
He'd bamboozled them quite a few years.
He was a crafty ole' polecat,
a gambler and rake of a man;
but one day the luck that came with him,
just packed up its suitcase and ran.

That day, Finney met with a stranger
who hadn't quite heard of him yet.
Finnegan flirted with danger
and challenged the man on a bet.
But the man wasn't cowed by his story
and failed to hold Finney in awe.
He knew naught of Finnegan's glory—
the talk of his lightening-quick draw.

He didn't back off...and he wasn't subdued....
and he sported the latest Colt gun.
Fast Finger floundered and came all unglued.
His legend was quickly undone.
The stranger was quick as greased lightening.
He left Finney flattened and dead.
He drew with a speed that was frightening,
and riddled poor Finney with lead.
The stranger was clearly fast-fingered
and Fast Finger clearly was not.
While the stranger's memory lingered,
Finnegan's face—they forgot.